Woven in the Details

Stories of the goodness of God
in our everyday lives

Melody R Stewart

ISBN: 978-1-7380304-0-8

DEDICATION

To my mother, Edith Louisa Binnie
who, by example, instruction and opportunity,
taught me to pray.

Her faith, woven into life's fabric,
is a generational legacy.

CONTENTS

ACKNOWLEDGMENTS

with Gratitude

For everyone who said, "You should write a book," well, I did! Thank you for your encouragement and motivation to pursue a dream that was tucked deep into a tiny corner of my heart and labelled - Next to Impossible. The One who gives us dreams didn't agree with that label. God kept bringing people into my life who would fan the flame of my dreaming a bit brighter, until eventually I began to write my stories. The more I wrote, the more I loved it. What a thrill it is to see this dream come to life.

To my four Beta Readers, (test readers who give feedback to an author's unpublished work) I value the time and insight each of you put into these stories to make them better. When more than one of you pointed out the same issue, I sure knew it needed to be fixed.

Tammy Resch, my better-together-friend at my side for eight years in Room E106. Your event planning abilities and my eagerness to help, created fun office memories. We were a great team helping each other with proofreading meeting minutes and email responses. Your keen eye for detail was still true to form in these stories. Thank you, my friend.

Sheila Stewart, the new niece I gained when I married into the Stewart clan! Knowing your professional editorial skills, I was equal-parts eager and nervous to ask you to help me out. I'm so glad I did. Your editing expertise was superb. It was very special for me to have a Stewart family member take part in this process. Thank you from the bottom of my heart.

My dear niece, Paula (Binnie) David, our shared DNA seemed to come through in your edits. Things you stated as unnecessary truly were. Your missionary and national office experience was very helpful. The warmth of your encouragement and prayers for the completion process was so meaningful to me. I'm glad Stephanie suggested I ask you. You represented the Binnie side beautifully and capably. Thank you.

Heather Gray, first a coworker, then a boss and, to my delight, a lifelong friend. It surprised me you wanted to be a beta reader, considering you've read my stories countless times before. In July 2020, the first story I sent you was a mere 637 words long. Without hesitation, you agreed to give me feedback. Your initial edits troubled me until I got over myself and saw the worth in them. I was such a rookie! By the time we had that first story stretched out like pizza dough, shaped properly, and layered with great toppings, it had doubled in size! Two years after that start, I'm eternally grateful for all that you have contributed to making this dream come true. You didn't just edit my work; you always included some encouragement which often made the difference in me carrying on or giving up.

You're a trailblazer and mentor to me in this publishing journey with your three books of realistic fiction published: The Lie, Where the Truth Lies and Consequences (see heatherdawngray.com). Your willingness to walk me through this process relieved me of a great deal of stress. I'm forever grateful to God for allowing our paths to cross and weaving some beautiful strands of life together in our stories. Thank you for your unwavering enthusiasm and support throughout this endeavour.

Shawn Henstridge, brother of Bessie, my first sister-in-heart, thank you for being a catalyst for me. When you told me a few years ago that *you* wrote a book (Things I Thought I'd Forgotten) and emphatically stated that I could write one too, you made me believe it was possible. Seriously! Thank you!

Betty Gould, your faithful prayers, encouragement, and phone calls were the support framework for this project. Not only did you pray, but you also followed up with phone calls to check in on me and even give me a good nudge when I needed it. Your love and friendship are priceless. I thank my God upon every remembrance of you!

To my children, Stephanie, Kyle, Heather, and Ruth, I'm so blessed to be your mom. You have enriched my life beyond belief. Our family fabric is strong, with life's joys and trials woven into our stories. What a beautiful tapestry it's become. Thank you each one for loving and cheering me on.

The required headshot-photo came together so easily. A regular appointment with my friend Sherry of Halo Hair Design gave me a fresh-cut smooth-hair look. Thank you, Sherry. My daughter Ruth came by the house after work and used her makeup-know-how magic on me. The second photo taken at the back door was *the one*! Thank you, Ruth, for such a stress-free process. Your ability to make ordinary-into-lovely is a gift and very much appreciated.

My dear sister, Sandra Zarn. For *all* the input and support you've given me on this project, I'm very thankful. Since childhood, I've admired your eye for beauty and your steadfast faith in God. Everything you said and did was fascinating to me. You were my first role model for all things girly and I'm so grateful God made us sisters. Realizing your piece of material was perfect for my book cover was such a fun moment. Thank you for that.

Kyle Stewart, thank you for taking my *okay* book cover and turning your version into something fabulous. Your expertise and attention to detail was over the top amazing. I'm thrilled with the outcome, especially since my own son made it for me!

My dear husband of forty-five years, Peter, for all the times I disappeared into the office and got lost for hours in the land of stories, thank you for having faith that I'd come back to the present eventually. When you read my first draft manuscript and cried, knowing you were touched by my words was like receiving a golden award. Your love and affirmation are essential to my heart.

To God, the one who gave me the love of stories and shows me the connecting threads, thank you for such undeserved love and guidance in my life. May these stories bring glory and honour to you. May the people who read them be blessed and see *you* woven in the details.

With love and appreciation from my heart, Melody

Preface

"Once upon a time" was all it took to get my attention. I've always loved stories. Without a television in our home growing up, the library was my source of entertainment. I'd read my adventure books with a flashlight under the covers when I was supposed to be sleeping. But I *had* to know how the story ended.

As the youngest child, family gatherings were always a source of fascinating stories. When my own children Stephanie, Kyle, Heather, and Ruth reminisce about family events, often the younger ones say, "I never knew that!"

An idea percolated in my heart and mind; what if I wrote down stories for my children and their children? As I began the process, it soon became clear that there was a familiar theme evolving. I already recognized God's hand in these events, but every detail further revealed his love and care. The closer I looked at the panoramic picture these stories painted, the more amazed I became.

God has been there for us in the good times and the bad. If you look closely at your own life, perhaps you too will see him in the details of your stories. If you don't see him but want him to be a part of your history, simply ask him in.

Woven in the Details is a collection of ten personal stories of our life and family. I invite you to read along and see the goodness of God in our everyday lives.

> Since my youth, God, you have taught me, and to this day I declare your marvelous deeds. Even when I am old and gray, do not forsake me, my God, till I declare your power to the next generation, your mighty acts to all who are to come.
>
> Psalms 71:17-18 NIV

Healing Tears

As I placed the telephone receiver on its cradle, my sweaty palm print was a visible indicator of how I was feeling. I made a beeline to the heart of our home to tell Mom about the phone call. Bread slices in columns lined the counter as she made lunches for Dad and a brother or two.

I knelt on the chair on the far side of the counter, my chin resting on my hands, and the words tumbled out. "Mom, I was just asked to share my healing testimony with the ladies' group at the Georgetown church."

Mom glanced up at me and smiled. "That's quite an honour! Some of those ladies prayed for you when you were sick. Did you agree to do it?"

"I did, even though the thought of talking in front of a group of people is terrifying! Whenever I present something in front of the class at school, my mouth goes dry, my hands shake, and I talk way too fast! But, since people like Mrs. Norton will be there, I really felt I should do it." I turned and sank down on the chair. I was trying not to be overwhelmed at the prospect of speaking in front of these older women but being seventeen years old and shy, I was failing miserably.

"That's a good way to look at it," Mom reassured me. "They won't care that you're not a polished speaker. They just want to hear your story."

"I hope so." I shrugged and sighed. I suddenly thought of a practical idea and quickly sat up. "Mom, I don't remember much about when I was healed, because I was too young. I heard the story many times, but it would help me tell it properly if I could write it down. Can you help me with that now?"

"Sure. I can do this and talk at the same time."

I jumped off the chair and ran upstairs to get a pencil and notebook before hurrying back to the kitchen.

I sat down at the table. "I'm all set. Can I ask you questions and write your answers?"

Mom's smile was encouraging. "Sure. That's a good idea."

With pencil in hand, I turned to Mom and started with the most basic question. "How old was I when I got sick?"

Mom finished buttering the bread, reached for the sliced meat and began to tell me "my healing story" as she'd told so many times before.

"Well Melody, when you were three years old, you began to complain of pains in your knees and ankles. Strange red spots started appearing all over your arms, legs, and hips. It looked like someone had thrown strawberries at you. They changed colour from red to blue, then brown, and faded away in three or four days."

"What made you decide to take me to the doctor?"

"When you told us your back hurt, we called the doctor's office. We didn't take you there as Dr. Garrett made a house call to see you. He told us the spots were purpura, which are small blood vessels that burst under the skin. He said you needed to go to the hospital for some tests, so on September 24th, 1962, we took you to Guelph General Hospital where you were admitted right away."

Mom collected her thoughts and then continued. "We'd go see you every day. Some days you'd be running up and down the halls. Other days, you were lifeless, just lying in your bed. I remember asking the nurse one day, 'When is Melody going to get to come home? The nurse's response caught me by surprise. 'Not for a long time.' she gravely replied."

"Did the doctor tell you what caused all the problems I was having?"

"Dr Garrett told us they were thinking it might be leukemia - cancer in the blood. The tests showed more white blood cells than red ones which is a sign of leukemia."

I wrote as fast as I could to get these details down.

Mom finished making the sandwiches and tidied up the counter.

"The day after the doctor told us about leukemia, we received a phone call from the Guelph hospital telling us we had to take you to Sick Children's Hospital in Toronto. You had been in Guelph for eleven days by then. Your dad had already gone to work up the road, so I had to phone the office to tell him to come home right away. Apparently, you had hemorrhaged three times from your bowels and had been sick to your stomach three times as well. Things were looking grim for you."

"That makes me feel oddly shaky inside hearing how sick I was. It must've been scary for you to hear that news from the hospital. Driving to Toronto always seems so far from here. Any idea why they didn't send me by ambulance?"

Mom joined me at the table with the tea towel in her hands. She folded it until it was a small rectangle and kept smoothing it as she talked.

"It sure stretched our faith. We knew then you were a *very* sick little girl and Toronto was close to a two-hour drive away. Ambulances were not routinely used or even covered by insurance back then so driving you to the hospital was not an unusual request."

"I'm sure you asked for prayer that day."

Mom's head came up and her eyes now glowed with passion. "Oh, yes! We were between ministers at church, but our church family had been praying for you already. I called Vivian Barker and asked her to call the other women of the church. Vivian told me later that they got right down on their knees and sought the Lord for your healing. Nellie Norton told me her tears soaked her sofa as she prayed for you."

That was always so humbling to hear. "I love hearing that part about Mrs. Norton's sofa. To think that all those people cared so much to pray so hard! For me!" I shifted in my chair, willing the lump in my throat to dissolve.

"Okay, tell me about the trip to Toronto!"

Mom smiled knowingly. "We'd just been listening to the teachings of T. L. Osborn, who believes it's always God's desire to heal us. By the time we arrived at the hospital in Guelph, I had a real peace in my heart, knowing the church ladies were praying for you. When the nurses brought you out to the car in front of the hospital, I had to look closely to see if you were even breathing. Your skin and even your lips were paper white, and you didn't move at all. One nurse gave us a flannelette sheet to spread across the backseat. They gave us blankets, some plastic bags, and extra sheets. They told us we would have an awful time because they were sure you would throw up and hemorrhage as we drove. Their last words were that we *must rush you* to the Sick Children's Hospital."

There was a catch in Mom's voice as she spoke.

"One other thing they provided us with was a child-size cup of ice water."

"Now, for the best part!" I urged Mom along.

"This is the beginning of the miracle part!!" she resumed, with warmth in her voice. "When they laid you down in the backseat, you didn't move. As we drove along, I kept checking over my shoulder to make sure you were okay. A short while later, I heard a little sound from you. In a whispery voice, you asked for a drink of water. I was so grateful for that cup of water! I gave you a little drink, and you settled again. But a little while later, you asked for another drink. You had several little drinks, and your voice got stronger each time. Eventually, you sat up and started happily playing with toys."

"That really must've been a surprise to you, since I looked so sick when we left."

"It was simply amazing. You seemed lifeless when we started out but as we drove you became strong and happy again. In fact, at the Toronto hospital, you looked so good, we had to wait a half hour before you got admitted. We bought you some ginger ale while you sat on the stretcher playing. Apparently, they had more urgent cases than you!"

"What happened once I was admitted to the hospital?" I asked.

"Because you were sent by another hospital, they had to run tests and give treatments according to what information they had. Tests were run for about a week and a half. Finally, those tests showed nothing wrong. During that time though, you caught a virus.

Mom's voice took on a brittle edge to it when she added, "Your time there is, in some ways, the hardest part of this story."

"Why's that, Mom?" I didn't enjoy hearing such sadness in her tone.

Mom absently wrote on the tea towel with her finger. Then she smoothed the towel again, as if to erase the words she wrote.

"Well, in those days, parents could _not_ stay with their child at the hospital. It was awful to have to leave you there, and you didn't understand what was happening or how far we were from home. I came back to visit as often as I could, staying all afternoon and evening if possible. Every time I visited, you would cling to me and when it came time for me to leave, you would cry hysterically and wrap yourself around me, holding on for dear life. The nurses had to pry you off so I could leave. I was crying as hard as you."

A lump formed in my throat and my eyes burned with tears at hearing how hard this had been on Mom.

"After one such visit, a nurse told me it would be better for you if I didn't come back and visit for a while. I'm sure they thought it would be better for me too, as we were both so upset at going-home time. When you caught the virus, you ended up in quarantine so I couldn't come for three weeks."

I wiped my eyes to clear my vision. "Thankfully Mom, I don't really remember that, probably because it was so awful!"

"What do you remember about your time in the hospital?" Mom asked me.

I had no trouble recalling a couple of things. "I remember my doll fell on the floor one day when the nurse was in the room. She picked it up and told me she had to sterilize it. I didn't know what that meant, but I wasn't happy about it as I kept waiting for her to bring my doll back. She never did. Likely it melted in the sterilizing process!"

Mom shook her head in sympathy. "That could be what happened! Do you remember anything else?"

"Yes, I do! A little boy in the bed beside me, had his legs hung up in the air with wires and metal poles. I didn't understand why that was, but now I know his legs were in traction. Poor kid! One day one of his toy soldiers fell on the floor. I hurried out of my bed, picked it up, and gave it back to him. I didn't want his toy to get taken away and never come back!"

Mom laughed. "I'm sure he appreciated you doing that for him!"

"He likely did," I agreed. "My turn again. Did anyone else come with you to the Toronto hospital to visit me?"

"Yes, your dad came when he could, and I was glad when he was doing the driving to Toronto. One time your sister Sandra came with me. She was fifteen and visitors had to be twelve years or older to visit back then. It was very hard on her to see you not looking like your normal self. Your hair was limp and dry looking. You had swollen cheeks, and you were not the cheery little girl she knew. She saw how upset you were when we had to leave, and that really bothered her too. When she went into Nursing School a few years after your healing, she learned that doctors sometimes used cortisone to treat leukemia. She also found out that a side effect of that medication was the 'moon face' like you had."

"That certainly would have been a shock to see me looking so awful." I hadn't thought about what it was like for Sandra to see me like that. I was impressed that she connected that information when she was training to be a nurse to when I was sick.

Mom added, "Your brothers were too young to visit. Archie was eleven, Brian was ten and

Jonathan was only 5 and had just started kindergarten. Sandra and other family members helped look after them when I was with you."

"How long was I in the Hospital for Sick Children?"

"The Toronto hospital admitted you on October 5th and discharged you on November 6th, so that was 33 days. When we include the length of time you were in the Guelph hospital, you were hospitalized for a total of six weeks and a day."

"Wow!" I breathed out softly.

"When we could finally bring you back home, I bought you a pair of white leotards to wear." She smiled as she recalled that. "I wrote in my diary: 'We find Melody is completely well.' Your brother Brian came with us to get you. He remembered watching you cross the lobby holding a doll. Apparently, one of the nurses bought you a new doll to take home. You were rather mystified when we arrived since you hadn't seen any of us for three whole weeks!"

"That's bizarre you couldn't come and see me for that length of time. That's a long time in a little kid's life!" The thought sent a shudder through me.

Mom sighed, cleared her throat, and leaned forward before she continued. "It was terrible being away from you all that time." Mom's eyes welled with tears again. "When you came home, you didn't let me out of your sight for almost two weeks. You followed me like a shadow wherever I went."

"I can believe that!" I replied. "Just like my doll had disappeared, I likely thought you would too!"

Mom paused briefly and then added in a husky voice, "It truly was a miracle that we could bring you home again. Sometime later, I had taken a friend and her daughter to the Guelph General Hospital when a nurse came up to me and asked if I was Melody Binnie's mother. When I told her I was, she asked how you were. She was astonished when I told her you were fine. She said, 'I can't understand it. We didn't expect you to get her to Toronto alive that day.'"

I shook my head and whispered, "That's completely incredible!!"

"Four years later, spots covered your body again, so I called the doctor's office about it. I didn't want to take you there if you were contagious, as measles were going around. Instead, to our surprise, Dr Garrett made an immediate house call. After a thorough checkup, he said it amazed him that your spots were only the German measles. He was likely expecting to see purpura again!"

I laid my pencil down as a tear fell on my paper. The magnitude of this miracle filled me with awe. I reached across the table for a tissue to wipe my eyes. A memory surfaced.

"I remember Dr Garrett coming to our house that time! He had that black doctor's bag where he kept his stethoscope. He had a nice deep voice, and he was so tall. I watched him leave and "fold himself" into his Volkswagen Beetle!" This fun memory was a relief after such an emotionally charged healing story.

I thought we had finished but Mom quickly added, "There's one more part to this testimony the ladies would like to hear. It's about your hair."

Holding my pencil over the pages now filled with my scribbled writings, I exclaimed, "Oh, yes! Tell me so I can write it down."

"Your hair was awful for quite some time after you came home. I didn't even like touching it because it felt dead." Mom looked down, as if embarrassed to admit to me how she felt.

"Not long after you came home during our Women's Ministry meeting, Mrs. Norton asked for prayer requests and started off by saying that we should pray for Melody's hair. More prayers went up and soon your hair came back to life. Just look at how thick and wavy it is even now." Mom smiled at me as she spoke.

"It's so great to hear all this again. It's as if I have a reminder anytime I brush my hair that God made me *all* better! Thank you so much, Mom. For everything."

We both rose from the table, and I hugged her tightly. Her unwavering faith was a source of strength and comfort to me. A priceless role model for my life.

~~~~~~~~~~~~~~~~~~~~~~~~

At the time of this writing, I'm in my early sixties, blessed with good health, am happily married, with four children, and seven grandchildren.

Even though my hair colour has changed from brown to grey, it is still thick and wavy and full of life. It is my ever-constant reminder of the goodness of God, of the power of prayer, and of the blessings of holding onto faith in God's word even when facing the impossible.
~~~~~~~~~~~~~~~~~~~~~~~~

Noteworthy:

I pondered how to write this story sixty years after the fact in a way that wouldn't just dump information on the page. Various unsuccessful attempts were made, until a memory surfaced of when I *was* invited to speak at the Women's Ministries group in the neighbouring town. Suddenly I had a true starting point.

From my own recollection of hearing the story and through many conversations with my sister Sandra, who has a phenomenal memory, the details were woven into this setting. Archie and Brian also shared memories of when I was sick.

Between writing, editing, and feeling the pressure of trying to get the story just right, I decided to take a break. A great procrastination opportunity in the shape of a box labelled Melody's Stuff, was sitting in my office waiting to be purged. For years.

This box had been to BC, Ontario and sat for more than a decade in Alberta. It had paper junk from the olden days and recent ones. I grabbed a full plastic bag on top of the pile and determined purging that bag would make me feel as though I accomplished something.

Part way through the bag, I pulled out a couple of pieces of lined paper with pencil writing on them. It took a moment to recognize the handwriting, but suddenly the words came into focus, and I realized what I was seeing.

My very own original notes from my teenage years, that I wrote when my mother told me my healing story once again.

Now THAT'S a God thing!

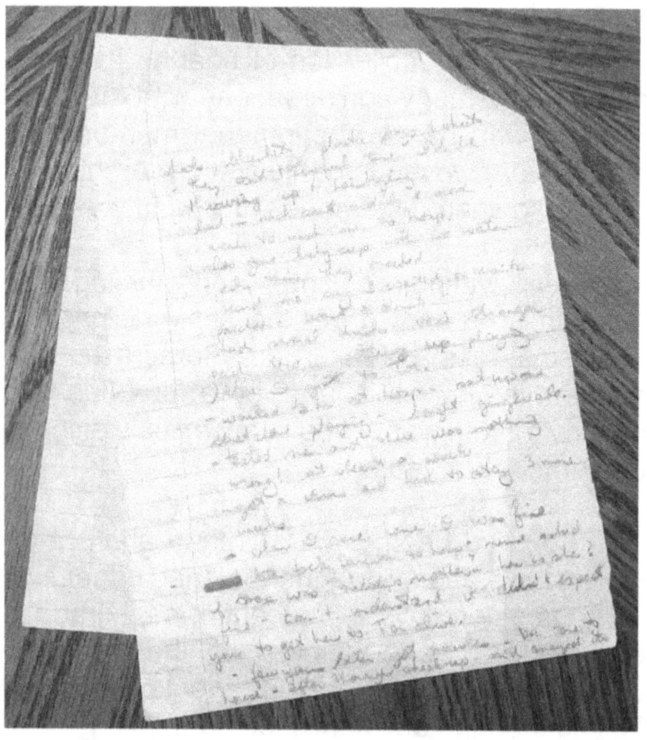

To the Rescue

In the middle of six lanes of traffic on Highway 401 east of Toronto, our trusty K-car station wagon lost acceleration power. With only the momentum of my current speed, I edged over to the shoulder of the road and slowed to a stop. That's when the engine stalled and wouldn't start again. I had enough presence of mind to switch the hazard lights on as my nerves took over, and I shook and cried silently as the magnitude of my dilemma sank in.

In the back seat, Ruth, only 18 months old, slept soundly in her car seat, while Stephanie and her friend Holly huddled together giggling as nine-year-old girls do. Kyle aged seven and three-year-old Heather were asleep in the front bench seat. I slipped out of the car as quickly and quietly as I could. It was autumn 1990 and the crisp October wind made my teeth chatter and my hair whip around my face. I hunched my shoulders, attempting to block the wind from going down my neck. It was already dark at seven pm. Even though I didn't have a flashlight, I released the latch, propped the hood open, and stared into the darkness of the engine.

"God, I don't have a clue what to do. I need your help." I swiped at the tears that seeped out and rolled down my cheek. "Please help." I knew having the hood up signified a broken-down vehicle, but I couldn't see anything noticeably wrong as I shivered from the cold. Taking a deep, shuddering breath, I opened the car door and slid back in behind the wheel. All the children were awake now.

 "What's wrong with the car, Mom?" Kyle stared at me with his big brown eyes.

"I don't know Kyle. It's too dark to see anything. The car quit and won't start."

Stephanie piped up, asking what I wondered as well. "How are we going to get it fixed? When are we going to get home?"

To the left of us, the six lanes of traffic continually whizzed by, making me feel invisible. On the ditch side, a chain-link fence topped with barbed wire surrounded a factory. The grounds were desolate on a Sunday evening.

If one of those 'Emergency Phones' was nearby along the highway, I wouldn't have noticed, as I was intent on navigating the traffic and getting home.

I weighed the options. I couldn't go for help leaving the kids in the car any more than I could send the older kids for help. Traipsing five children along the expressway until the next sideroad was out of the question, especially in the dark.

"Listen kids," I struggled to keep the trembling from my voice, "I don't know how we're going to get the car fixed or how we'll get home. If Dad was here, he'd know. For now, we're safe on the side of the road."

The vulnerability of my situation made it hard to breathe. I did the one certain thing I knew to do. Composing myself, I continued. "No one knows where we are or that anything has happened to us except God. He's the only one who can help us, so we need to pray."

I prayed out loud to reassure myself as much as the children. "Dear Jesus, you see us on the side of the road in the middle of nowhere. It's dark, we're scared and have no way of getting help. Please send someone good to come and help us and keep us safe." My voice broke. "Amen." The children went quiet.

It had been such a good weekend in Acton, celebrating Mom's birthday with my two brothers and their families. She loved having us arrive at the house even with our chaos and noise. Peter's absence while in Taiwan for his two-month Bible College internship made me extra grateful to spend time with my parents and family. Their support helped me feel like I could keep going, without Peter, for another seven weeks. But now I needed him here. What did I know about fixing cars? Nothing. My stomach churned and tears burned behind my eyelids. I felt so helpless.

A long fifteen minutes passed when Stephanie's voice jolted me back to our plight. "Why doesn't God make someone stop?"

"I don't know," was the most truthful response I had.

Another long five minutes passed before brake lights appeared ahead, and a tow truck pulled over to the side of the road. It backed up in front of our car. I swung open the door and jumped out, then poked my head back in. "Stay in the car, kids. I'll be right back." I shut the door and hurried to meet the driver.

"Hello there. How can I help you?" His words were like music to my ears as he hopped down from his truck.

"Thank you so much for stopping! My car just began losing power as we were driving down the highway. It coughed and sputtered as I steered over to the shoulder. It came to a standstill and won't start now. I've got five kids here with me and we're going home to Peterborough." I knew I was rambling, but I couldn't stop myself. "Would you be able to take us somewhere that I could use a telephone? I can call some friends and I'm sure they'd come and get us." I took a deep breath and hoped this man would take pity on us.

"Are you sure you don't want me to take you to a garage? I should be able to find one still open."

The very thought horrified me. I knew I had CAA coverage, but I had no way of paying for garage repairs. "No thank you, just somewhere I can phone and wait for our friends."

"No problem. I can do that. Further down the highway is a place where the car can sit in the parking lot. We need to get it off this section of road. You'll all have to sit in the truck's cab, though. Nobody can be in the car while I'm towing it."

The kids were excited when I told them we were getting a ride in the truck. As I retrieved Ruth from her car seat, the older girls took Heather by the hand and followed Kyle, who led the way. Double-decker seating was the way to go. Kyle climbed in first and with much protest and laughter, Stephanie followed to sit on his lap. Holly hoisted Heather onto her lap as she slid in next to them. I handed Ruth up and climbed in last. As I shut the cab door, a great sense of relief washed over me. I was so grateful to not be stranded on the side of this highway any longer. Our rescuer did whatever was involved in hooking up our little red car and then he joined us.

"Is everybody comfortable?" he cheerfully asked.

A few giggles came in response and an honest 'no' from Kyle.

"I'm not actually on duty now," our driver shared as he peered over the children's heads. "I was coming home from a meeting when I saw your car with the hood up, so I had to check if you needed help."

He was dressed more business-like than a tow truck driver. His shoes even had tassels on them. It was satisfying to hear that leaving the hood up had sent out the right message.

Heading toward Whitby, our driver eventually exited onto a sideroad and pulled into a donut shop parking lot. The six of us spilled out of the cramped quarters and eagerly headed inside while our driver unhooked our vehicle.

As soon as my eyes caught sight of the wall payphone, I put Stephanie in charge of her siblings, lifted the receiver, and pushed the '0' button. When the operator answered, I heard those sweet words again, "How may I help you?"

"I'd like to make a collect-call to Laurie and Julie Howlett, please." As I rattled off their phone number, I prayed they were home. Julie answered, and I waited impatiently for my turn to speak. Julie's response to the operator's next question stood between me and potential help.

"I have a collect call from Melody Stewart. Will you accept the charges?"

At Julie's affirmative answer, the operator left the call, and I was free to pour out our story to Holly's mom. I asked if Laurie would consider coming to see if he could fix the car. Julie assured me she would track him down at the church, and they'd rescue us. Although we'd have to wait, help was on its way again.

As I hung up the receiver, the kids had happily taken over the donut shop. It was quite evident they were glad to be out of the car after such a long confinement. The tow truck driver stood by the door, patiently waiting to talk to me.

Approaching him with a sense of dread, I asked, "How do you want me to pay for the tow?"

"Do you have CAA coverage?" he asked. "I'll just send the bill to them."

Digging out my CAA card from my wallet, I handed it to him apologetically as I clarified my membership. "Yes, but we only have the 3-mile basic coverage." I knew we had gone a lot farther than that on our ride. "How much do I owe for the extra miles of towing?" I braced myself for his answer because I didn't have any idea how I'd pay for this either.

"Oh, that's alright. Don't worry about it." He gave me his business card and told me he lived just a few blocks away. "If your friends don't come or you need anything, just call. I'll be at home the rest of the evening." With that, he turned toward the door.

"Thank you so much. You're an answer to my prayer," I called out after him. He looked back and smiled.

I sank gratefully into the nearest chair as Ruth climbed onto my lap to drink her bottle of milk. This was turning into a long night for my little girl.

Our curly-haired Heather easily entertained other customers in her delightful, charming way. Stephanie and Holly sat at a table by themselves and drew pictures. Kyle tried to join in, but sometimes three is a crowd, so when he came sorrowfully back to me, I suggested he draw a picture of the tow truck and we would mail it to Daddy. He liked that idea and went right to work on his masterpiece. This late-night journey had taken its toll on him as he drew tears on his face standing beside the tow truck. He included the fact that the driver had an earring. When Kyle showed me his picture, he told me he kept praying after I did until the truck came. The faith of our seven-year-old boy impressed me.

When the Howletts arrived from Peterborough close to two hours later, we all simply wanted our beds. Laurie checked over the car and determined he needed a part to fix it, but the stores were now closed. We piled into their car for the final hour-long ride home. The last leg of the journey soon became quiet as the children succumbed to sleep. It was 11:15 when we were dropped off at our house. What was normally a two-hour trip home had expanded to a five-and-a-half-hour adventure.

The next day Laurie and his friend, Greg Clairmont, drove back to our car at the donut shop. After purchasing and changing the broken rotor under the distributor cap, they drove both vehicles back to Peterborough. I asked Laurie how much I owed him, and his reply lifted the lingering weight from my shoulders.

"There isn't any bill. It's all good."

Eventually I heard the part cost only seven dollars which was a relief. It touched my heart to discover Laurie, who was the custodian, had to work that evening at the church to make up for missing time getting my vehicle back.

God indeed sent the very best 'good' people to our rescue as we had prayed for. Calling the Howletts wouldn't have crossed my mind if Holly hadn't been with us. Even though they lived a few doors down the street, and we attended the same church, we mainly knew them as the parents of Stephanie's friend. They came so willingly, brought us all home, then went above and beyond to fix and return our car.

A knight in business-casual armour had showed up in his horse-powered tow truck, rescuing a damsel in distress with a carload of kids. Although I've forgotten his name, the name of his towing company stuck in my memory. Excalibur Towing. Suitable for a modern-day knight, with tassels on his shoes.

~~~~~~~~~~~~~~~~~~~~~~
~~~~~~~~~~~~~~~~~~~~~~

My mother died in 1993, just three years after writing a letter to my brother and sister-in-law, relaying this story of my adventure home. My sister-in-law gave me that letter a few years ago. When I sat down to write this story, I easily recalled the big picture, but a lot of the details were hazy. Then I remembered the letter. I dug it out and reread this account in my mother's own handwriting. The details were amazing and exactly what I needed. My mother would have acknowledged it as a 'God-thing' that her letter 'came to my rescue' over 30 years later.

Her closing words to Archie and Bessie reduced me to tears.

> "I'm thankful that Melody knows how to pray. I am thankful that our God is willing to hear and answer our prayers."

I learned to pray because my mother taught me to pray. Anytime, anywhere, for anything. I needed no telephone line to call heaven. Just a simple, ragged cry from my heart to His. And answer, He certainly did.

My precious carload:
Ruth, Holly, Kyle, Heather & Stephanie

My mother's handwritten words
to Archie and Bessie about my adventure.

Displaced Person

A mosaic of people filled the waiting room's vinyl chairs. A fellow with a deep blue turban and a long grey beard sat calmly on one side of me. A mother with a Caribbean accent tended to two young children nearby.

I couldn't help but notice one man wearing a long black robe with a small round hat on his head. He strode around the waiting area talking loudly on his cell phone in a language unfamiliar to me. His robe flapping loudly around his ankles matched the intensity of his conversation.

The drive to this government office in Mississauga was stressful for me. I had spent the last eleven years in British Columbia, eight of those in small northern communities with much less cross-cultural exposure and much more open space. Now, in 2002, I struggled to regain my footing in this frantic-paced metropolis with endless asphalt, high rises, industrial buildings, and shopping centers crowding my senses. Despite being close to my birthplace, reverse-culture-shock had taken hold of me. Instead of this area feeling like home, nothing seemed normal, and I was homesick for the familiar. I shifted uncomfortably in my seat. In my glumness, I tossed an honest question from my heart heavenward. "God, do _you_ even know where I am?"

"Melody Stewart, customer service counter five, please." The female voice with a strong British accent startled me out of my pity party. Sighing heavily, I stood and quickly walked toward her counter.

"I need a piece of government ID please," came the expected request, but it surprised me to realize the British accent belonged to a woman of East Indian ethnicity. I slid my driver's license across the counter to her.

She took my license in her hand, turning it over to the front where our previous Fort Nelson, BC address was listed. After verifying my name and photo, she smiled at me. "Fort Nelson. I've been to Fort Nelson."

I gasped as I tried to comprehend her matter-of-fact statement. "Really? You've been to Fort Nelson?"

Fort Nelson, with a population of 4500, sits at Mile 300 on the Alaska Highway with a push-button crosswalk as the only traffic control light. Fort Nelson, where a four-story walk-up is considered a high-rise apartment. And where black bears get into the garbage if you don't follow the garbage storage rules. What reason would this British woman from Toronto have for visiting Fort Nelson? I honestly didn't believe her.

"Oh yes. My husband has an engineering degree in mining. He received a job offer in Faro, Yukon, so we moved there from India."

I had presumed with her British accent she was from England. Hearing she moved to Canada from India caught me by surprise. I then realized India had a great deal of British influence over the years, so her accent from there did make sense.

It was her turn to be surprised though when I said, "I've been to Faro, Yukon."

"You have?"

"Yes. One summer, my husband and I with our two youngest daughters drove up north to explore the area. Faro certainly is in the middle of nowhere."

Faro was a much smaller community than Fort Nelson and a further eleven-and-a-half-hour drive north.

"Most people would go south to bigger centers, not north to the smaller ones!" she replied handing my license back.

"We always enjoy exploring less touristy places."

I was still trying to reconcile her homeland with her location in the north. "What an incredible change to move from India to a remote small town in northern Canada."

I opened my wallet to tuck my driver's license back in place. "The difference in temperature from India's heat to the brutal cold of northern winters would be shocking!"

She entered data into the computer and printed out forms. Her voice rang with laughter. "That's for sure! One winter, I bought a few groceries from the store. As I walked home, I heard a tinkling sound, and I couldn't figure out where it was coming from. When I got in my house, I found the grapes frozen and clinking together."

As she slid the papers to me to sign, she continued. "I didn't even bother to tell my parents because they wouldn't have believed me. They didn't know how people could actually survive such cold temperatures. I tried to tell them we had nice warm clothing like winter coats and boots, mitts, and scarves, but that was just as unbelievable to them as the cold itself!"

I laughed heartily at such a statement.

"That would've been too much for them to understand." After verifying the information and signing the form, I slid it back to her, shaking my head in sympathetic understanding.

"Moving from southern Ontario to northern British Columbia was like relocating to a completely different world within the same country. The distance between places and all the driving we did up north boggled my southern relatives' minds. We drove six and a half hours one way for our daughter's monthly orthodontist appointments. It became normal though. Now, being back here feels so weird."

"You'll adapt again," she reassured me. "All in good time. *We* did."

Her smile and encouraging words were like soothing lotion on rough skin.

My soul felt renewed by the time this woman finished reactivating my Ontario health coverage. Instead of feeling out of place, I'd met a kindred spirit who understood the complex feelings of being a displaced person.

Of all the wickets I could have been called to, I knew exactly why I was called to hers. God had answered my earlier skeptical prayer with a resounding, "Yes! Of course I know where you are!"

And he said it in the most delightful British accent.

A Spot to Rest

Mum Stewart's funeral was over but there was one last detail to take care of before flying back home to Alberta. Peter, Stephanie, Heather, Ruth, Peter's brother Doug and I were on the highway in our rental van with a specific goal in mind. As we turned off the highway south of Peterborough onto Boundary Road, Peter assured us we were close to our destination.

We followed the road toward the forest entrance. Symmetrically planted trees lined up in countless rows, evidence of a reforestation project years before. Now those trees towered well above the roadway, creating canopies of cool shade.

Earlier in the week, we had come to Ontario to celebrate Mum Stewart's life with the rest of the family, including the clan from the states. It had been a precious time, full of tears and laughter, grieving and reminiscing. We met new babies and in-laws and saw some of the people that Mum's life had touched.

Peter had been to this forest previously, thirty-one years ago with his Mum to spread Dad Stewart's ashes. This trip had a similar purpose. Nestled in the van in a simple cardboard container were Mum's ashes. She had requested them to be scattered close to her husband's.

Peter didn't find what he wanted on the side roads we passed.

"Where is that fire warden tower? I'm sure it's in this section of the forest." Peter muttered to himself. I could hear bewilderment edged in frustration in his voice. I leaned forward in my seat of the rental van, hoping that somehow the tower would appear in front of us.

Peter turned down another road. Still no tower in sight.

"We're going back to the entrance to figure out where to go. There was a sign that could be useful back there."

If Peter can't find his way with his built-in GPS-mind, that's a problem.

We all scoured the horizon for any sign of a tower as Peter drove back to a billboard displaying a forest map. Pulling to a stop, we all climbed out of the van eager to look at the map, hoping to see fire tower locations. The sign showed the general area with dirt bike trails marked throughout the forest, along with the rules and regulations for using the trails. Sadly, there was no sign of fire warden tower locations at all.

A pickup truck pulled over and a young man and boy joined us, also staring at the sign.

Peter approached them and cleared his throat. "Excuse me. Do you know where the fire warden tower is?"

"Sorry man. This is my first time here. My son and I are going dirt-biking."

"Thanks anyway. Enjoy your time together." Peter took a last glance at the sign and shook his head in resignation. Following his lead, we all quietly climbed back into the van. A sense of dismay permeated the air.

Peter turned onto the main road again and passed the side road we had been on before.

"I'm sure this is not the right direction, but maybe I missed the turnoff."

Knowing the time was passing, and it was a two-hour drive back to Doug's home, the pressure to find the tower increased. There didn't seem to be any other way to find the information we needed and no matter which direction we drove, there was no tower to be seen.

I stated the obvious. "We need to pray." I figured I would just tell God our problem, as we were out of options. "God, please help us find this tower because it's important to us for Mum. Today is our last chance to be here before we leave tomorrow. You know where we need to go. Please show us the way. Thank you. Amen."

Checking down various other sideroads as we travelled on the main road, none of them looked right either. In exasperation, Peter hit the steering wheel with the palm of his hand. "I know we're going the wrong direction, so I'm going back the way we came." He pulled over, once more prepared to turn around.

As he did, a white dusty pickup truck with a dirt bike in the back appeared from a side road on our left. The driver's window was down, and his arm rested on the door, but it was his long grey beard and grey ponytail that caught my attention.

He caught Peter's attention too, as he lowered his window and waved at the man in the truck, beckoning him over to us. "Maybe this guy knows the forest better!"

The driver slowed down and then turned towards us, pulling up alongside the van. "Hey, how's it going?"

"Hi there. We're hoping you might help us. We're trying to find the fire warden tower. Would you know where it is, by any chance?"

He answered with a question. "The new tower or the old one?"

I gasped. *He knows! I'm sure he does.*

"The _old_ one," was Peter's quick and certain response.

"You bet I know it. Turn around and take the fifth road from the entrance. Go up around the corner, to a gravel laneway on the right. Pull in there and park."

We were all listening intently.

"There's a steep hill to walk up, but at the top will be the cement bases of that tower. Years ago, the old tower was demolished and another one was built in the new section."

My eyes filled with tears at this wonderful news. Our destination was close now.

The gloomy atmosphere dissipated. The girls were laughing and chattering together. We were all shouting our thanks to him as he prepared to leave. I called out before he was out of hearing range, "What's your name?"

"Michael," came the reply and a wave.

"Of course it is! Thank you, Michael! You're an angel!" I hollered as he left in a trail of dust.

The correct side road was one over from where Peter had first turned. His big brown eyes now sparkled in the mirror as he declared, "No wonder I couldn't see the tower. It wasn't just hidden by trees. I knew the spot I was looking for was near here!"

I smiled, knowing his GPS-mind was still intact.

Without the pressure to find the tower, we appreciated the beauty of the forest. Regal pine trees lined up row by row on each side of the dirt road until they merged into a wall of green in the distance. Trilliums, the lovely provincial flower of Ontario, carpeted the forest floor.

As we rounded the corner, the short gravel lane appeared to our right. We drove to the foot of the hill and parked the van. Stepping out into the peacefulness of the forest, the noise of our feet crunching on the loose stone path seemed out of place.

Peter carried the special box as he reminisced with Doug about the time they had visited there as a family when they were young. He shared details with us. "We climbed the ladder right to the top of the fire tower. The ladder had a wire cage around it that made it awkward to climb, but it kept us safe from falling backwards. When we made it to the top, there was a roof covered platform. The walls had openings instead of windows."

"What was the view like?" I asked.

"It was incredible! You could see above the treetops for miles and miles in every direction. I'll never forget that sight."

"Did you climb it any other time?"

"No, only once. The ladder caging had a lock on it the next time we came."

"Hmm, but what a great memory of that view."

As we reached the top of the steep hill, we were rewarded with the sight of the cement bases of the tower, just as Michael had described.

Peter scanned the area surrounded by trees so tall that we couldn't see past them. Choosing a nearby tree, he knelt at its base. Opening the small box, then the inner package, Peter gently poured Mum Stewart's ashes onto the ground. He remained there silently for a time with Doug nearby as the rest of us stood a distance behind.

We each took our turn at the base of the tree, paying our last respects. I thanked God again for the amazing mother-in-law He had blessed me with. Her wonderful sense of adventure, her unconditional love for her family, and the way she quietly went about doing good for others, all had impacted my life profoundly. I loved her so much.

I looked around this setting. It was obvious why Mum wanted this as her final earthly resting place. She loved the tranquility of the woods; she loved beautiful flowers, and the memories of good times spent in this forest with her husband and family. It was a perfect spot to rest.

A spot to rest we found thanks to the help of a grey-haired angel with a ponytail.

Fire Warden Tower Bases

A spot to rest

No Interpretation Needed

I craned my neck to see if there were any seats available as the bus approached. The feeble morning sun and dim interior lights illuminated most spaces were already occupied. My only thought when I boarded the bus each day was to find somewhere to sit quickly and quietly, drawing as little attention to myself as possible.

Even on this early bus, there were very few places to sit. One older Asian woman occupied an aisle seat with a space next to the window. On this day, I stopped beside her, pointed to the spot, and asked, "May I sit here?" Without saying a word, she simply turned her knees to the aisle and let me in. She had a cane tucked between the seats, so I wondered if she had mobility challenges. I was content simply to be her seat buddy. After thanking her I reached into my bag for my book.

The next morning, I boarded the well-filled bus behind another passenger. I expected it to be standing-room-only at the back door as she led the way ahead of me. Mid-way to the back, that same Asian lady sat on the aisle seat. She did not move as the woman ahead of me passed, but as soon as I reached her, she quickly moved her legs out into the aisle to let me into the window seat. What a sweet surprise.

I thanked her again. She patted my hand and leaned closer. "You read."

With a chuckle, I pulled out my book as before.

The next time I got aboard, she was watching for me, with a ready smile, and it became apparent the vacant seat was for me. Thereafter, we would happily sit together and began trying to communicate.

I told her my name and wrote it down for her. She pointed below the handle of her cane to her name written in both Chinese and English and said, "Wei Yin." Pointing at me, she asked, "How old?"

"I'm fifty." I replied, even as I wrote it down on paper. She took my paper to write 81 on it. We were over thirty years apart in age. Noting the very few strands of gray in her hair, I shook my head, saying, "Wow! You do not look your age." She laughed at my disbelief and nodded at the number she had written.

We continued to communicate with her broken English and my limited Mandarin. I knew just a couple of phrases: Ni Hao Ma (how are you) and Xie Xie (thank you). Gestures, writing things down, and even my attempts to draw pictures produced much laughter and enjoyment on our early morning journeys.

A large group of us, including my seatmate, would exit the bus close to downtown and head across the street toward Grant MacEwan College. Other riders and I would veer right to a bus shelter to continue our journey while she disappeared into the institution with the rest.

I wondered what she did at Grant MacEwan. Teach, take classes, work? One day as we crossed the road, I asked her, "What do you do there?" pointing to the building in front of us.

She said something I couldn't understand and swung her arms back and forth in front of her to explain. I wondered if she was showing cleaning motions, but that made no sense knowing her age.

Another bus passenger overheard our attempts to communicate, and she clarified Wei Yin's actions for me "She goes swimming!"

My eyes widened in surprise! My new friend was so dedicated. I could barely get motivated in the morning to get to work on time and she was up before the sun to go swimming! I laughed in delight.

I fell in love with this sweet lady. Eventually, as we parted ways, I would give her a hug, which she readily accepted.

In mid-October Wei Yin announced, "I go Taiwan."

My heart skipped a beat, then pounded faster at the thought of her absence.

Oh, no! "To live? Vacation?"

Her quick response of "Vacation. Next week," made me breathe a sigh of relief. It was a temporary separation. I wanted to let her know how much she meant to me before she left. The rest of the way to work and on into my morning routine, I pondered what I could do. With only a few days before she would be gone, I needed to figure this out quickly.

Finally, I decided on an idea that would involve some outside help. The next day, I brought my little red digital camera with me. As we crossed the road together, I pulled the camera out of my bag, pointed to her and then myself, and asked if I could take our picture. She nodded with a smile.

With the camera turned around, we took our first selfie photo. It took a few tries, but eventually, both of our faces fully appeared in the photo. I hugged her goodbye and headed off to catch my next bus.

At work, I had the photo printed at the Project Factory on a full sheet of paper, leaving room for a specific message already written in my mind. As the Program Assistant in the Medical Laboratory Technology program, I knew of a mature student who came from China. Even though he spoke Cantonese, the written words were similar in both languages. I tracked him down between classes and asked if he would write my message in Chinese beside my English text. He agreed and wrote what, hopefully, was a close translation:

> Melody and Wei Yin understand the
> language of friendship.

On the next ride together, as I settled into my favourite reserved place beside my friend, I pulled out my card and tucked it in her hands. With a slight furrow in her brow, she opened it and saw the four photo attempts with our partial faces, she laughed. As she read the words, a warm smile lit up her face. She squeezed my hand and said, "Thank you. Xie Xie."

As we rode together that last time before her trip back home, my heart weighed with sadness thinking about her upcoming absence from my life. While I processed my feelings, Wei Yin drew my attention to the zipper pull of a little cross on her handbag. She cradled the cross in her hand and clearly said, "Jesus, in my heart."

My eyes welled up with tears at this surprising declaration, and with great excitement I replied, "Me too!" I reached into my bag to pull out my book. It was a Max Lucado Daily Bible. Every page had the cross symbol on the header. I pointed to the cross and then covered my heart. "Me too!"

It's no wonder we enjoyed each other's company. We were spiritual sisters.

I only saw Wei Yin a few times after she returned from her six-month vacation in Taiwan. Perhaps it became too hard for her to go swimming anymore. I still miss her sweet smile and warm friendship, but I know someday we will meet again. After a big, long hug, we will have all of eternity to reminisce.

No interpretation needed.

Melody and Wei Yin
understand the language
of friendship.

友情就是我们之间的
语言.

Melody 赠 Wei Yin

From Siberia with Love

I stepped out of the penthouse guest suite and gazed up at the towering apartment buildings surrounding this mere five-story one. The incredible city of Hong Kong - the farthest I'd ever been from home and my first overseas trip - saturated my senses with wonder and amazement. With only two days left of our 2015 vacation to savour, I headed across the rooftop to the Winsor's penthouse apartment to join Peter for breakfast.

As I entered the small dining-living room, I saw Peter with Murray Cornelius, a fellow Canadian whom we'd met the night before, at the breakfast table. Our hosts were already at work in their office.

Peter grinned as he announced, "Murray and I figured out who else besides your brother we know in common. A missionary family, the Bantseevs!"

I laughed with delight at the game we play when we meet people from somewhere we are familiar with. Murray was here on business from Mississauga, Ontario just for the weekend and since we had relatives there, this met the game criteria to see if we knew the same people.

"That's awesome! Good morning, Murray!" I smiled remembering the Bantseevs as I helped myself to the hearty western-styled breakfast and joined them at the table.

"Good morning," Murray greeted cheerfully as he turned back to Peter, "So, did you see the Christmas video they sent last month?"

"No, we haven't heard from the Bantseevs in years. We knew of their missionary work in the late 90's and briefly met them in 2002 while staying with Melody's brother Brian, in Mississauga."

"Oh, you must see this video! It's powerful. I'll get my laptop so you can watch it while you eat. It's just something else!"

And with that, since there was no elevator in this old building, Murray hurried out the door and down the 114 stairs to his guest room on the ground floor.

We both finished our breakfast and were enjoying another coffee when Murray returned. The finicky internet delayed the setup, but once the video started, Murray told us to enjoy it, and with a wave, headed off to a meeting.

The polite obligation we felt as we watched the Christmas video soon dissolved into fascination. After a brief greeting by Ilya and Janet Bantseev, the camera switched to focus on the people they had helped. These men and women solemnly recounted their previous lives of addiction, despair, and hopelessness. But their eyes lit up and their voices rang with joy as they spoke of their complete transformation.

The changes began when they met this missionary family who had moved to Novokuznetsk, Siberia and introduced them to Jesus. In a country where alcohol and drug addictions are prevalent in every sphere of life, the Bantseevs goal was to bring help and hope. They had set up Teen Challenge Centers providing year-long faith-based rehabilitation programs for men and women. Once freed from addiction's stranglehold, these people experience a new purpose in life and a sense of belonging with fellow believers.

These testimonies of dramatic life changes thrilled my heart. Growing up in church, I'd heard similar stories all my life. They were as exciting to hear now as when I was a child.

What caught me by surprise was the emotional reaction I had to the closing statement each person made. "Thank you for sending the Bantseevs to us. Thank you for your part in helping us get to know Jesus." My heart thudded in surprise as I heard this for the first time. When the second person expressed their gratitude, my vision blurred. By the time the last one repeated similar words, tears poured down my cheeks and a sob escaped as the video ended. I glanced at Peter, who was also wiping away tears as he closed the laptop.

"They were thanking us too," he choked out.

"Yes! That's exactly what I was thinking!"

We couldn't help but reflect on our initial long-distance connection with the Bantseev family that began many years ago.

~~~~~~~~~~~~~~~~~~~~~~~

We had arrived in Fort Nelson, BC in the spring of 1994 to pastor a little church struggling to survive. The congregation had dwindled, and the bills had mounted in recent times. An interim retired pastor and his wife had kept the church
~~~~~~~~~~~~~~~~~~~~~~~

going until they could find a permanent pastor. When Peter took over as pastor our focus with the faithful few was to make sure the bills were paid and necessary repairs to the building were taken care of. As the congregation increased in numbers, they began looking beyond themselves to helping others.

In 1997 a board member suggested that our church give an additional monthly portion of the general offerings to support a specific missionary family. With the congregation's approval, Peter requested information about missionaries from the church's national office. They emailed a simple list of names and addresses back to him. One address in Siberia caught Peter's attention since we were living in a northern district of Canada. Curious about their location, Peter scanned a map, only to discover they were south of Fort Nelson in latitude.

Novokuznetsk is a centuries-old city of half a million people with a large iron plant and coal mine industry. Ilya Bantseev, a Russian-born immigrant to Canada, had recently returned to his hometown of Novokuznetsk, Siberia, with his wife and young son to start a church there.

Peter shared the family's information with our church congregation, and they embraced this connection as fellow northerners.

Our church giving, combined with other supporters, provided an income for the Bantseevs as they pursued their calling to help the people of Siberia. We were informed by email of ministry updates and prayer requests for various situations they faced.

The Banseevs were often forced to move their church service location because of government and religious opposition. Eventually, they rented a room in an old shoe factory with no heat or running water. Having their own building would be very beneficial to them.

The national office purchased a prefabricated steel building, capable of accommodating 500 people and transported it from Canada to Siberia in shipping containers. A piece of land had been given to the ministry but when the shipping container arrived, the authorities initially refused to give permission to use the building. After two years of negotiating, praying, and waiting, approval finally came to use it as a sports center for their work with youth and eventually to hold Sunday church services too.

Our little church in the northeast corner of British Columbia faithfully prayed for and sent money to support this courageous family for close to four years.

~~~~~~~~~~~~~~~~~~~~~~
~~~~~~~~~~~~~~~~~~~~~~

Sitting in an apartment in Hong Kong, watching their video filled us with joy. Peter and I were inspired to hear how the Bantseev's ministry in Siberia flourished despite the hardships they faced. Learning that multiple addiction rehabilitation centers had been successfully established and the missionaries were fully accepted by the people whose lives had changed, encouraged our hearts. The knowledge that our little church family played a part in their ministry reaffirmed how amazing it is to follow the prompting of God.

It wasn't until six months later, back home in Edmonton, Alberta, that this story truly came full circle. Friends we met in Fort Nelson, Wayne and Linda Peckford, visited us from outside the province. We talked about God's faithfulness and how He weaves life's details together. We told them about Murray and the video of the Bantseevs he had shown us.

I turned to Peter. "Who was it that suggested our church support a missionary family?"

He looked somewhat puzzled as if I should know the answer. With a nod of his head toward our friend, he confirmed, "It was Wayne's idea."

"Wayne! They thanked _you_ too! Those people's lives changed dramatically because you listened to God's nudge in your heart."

Wayne, in his typical self-effacing way, shrugged his shoulders and averted his eyes. "Really? Right on, man. Right on."

We all burst out laughing, as it certainly was "right on" indeed.

Eighteen years later, the harvest of a simple suggestion came to rest with the very person who planted the seed. Wayne learned of the impact of his idea because Peter and I watched a Christmas video in January in Hong Kong!

A video that came from Siberia, with love!

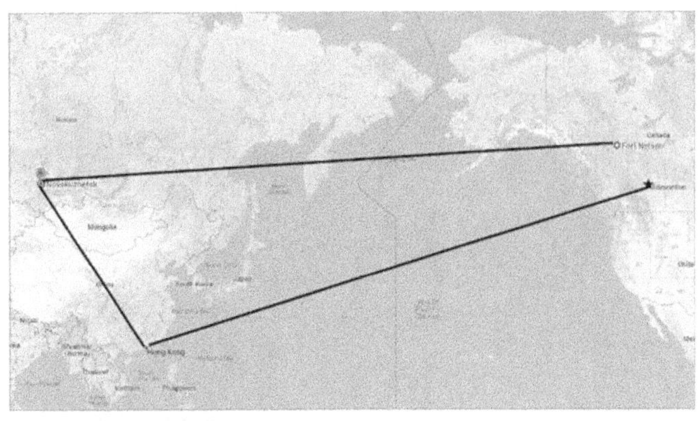

Connections

From Fort Nelson, BC
To Novokuznetsk, Siberia
To an apartment in Hong Kong
To Edmonton
It's a God thing!

Wayne & Linda Peckford, Melody & Peter

Made with Love Anonymously

My cell phone rang just as I sat down with a fresh cup of coffee. Grateful for the distraction from my to do list, I reached across my desk and quickly snatched up my phone before it could ring again.

"Hi Mom." Hearing Stephanie's voice made me smile. "I was hoping to tell you about the Ladies Spring 2012 Conference this weekend! Is this a good time?"

"It's perfect. I'm having my coffee break, and no one's around now." I settled back in the chair and took a delicious sip. "How did it go?"

"It was really great!" The enthusiasm in her voice matched her words. "The theme of the conference was 'Love Mercy' from the verse in Micah 6:8."

"Oh, that's a great verse."

> *What does the Lord require of you? To act justly and to love mercy and to walk humbly with your God.*

I smiled as I quoted it to myself.

"Yeah, it is. The last session on Saturday really made me think. The speaker discussed how doing acts of love or kindness for people is easy when we know they will appreciate it. When we see how happy we've made them, it makes us feel good."

"Hmm, that's true, isn't it? That kind of reaction seems to motivate us to keep doing those sorts of things."

"Absolutely. The speaker challenged us to do something for others without recognition. A selfless act mercifully given."

I sat up straighter in the chair and mused. "That was quite a challenge! It would make you stop and think!"

"It really did." Her voice took on a serious tone as she explained the details. "The speaker asked us to take a few minutes to think about the challenge, to pray and ask God what He would want us to do."

I was eager to hear where this conversation was going. "What happened next?"

"When we got an idea, we were supposed to write it down on a blank card left on our seats at the beginning of the day."

I walked down the hallway to the lunchroom with my coffee in one hand and the phone in the other, as if movement would help me hear the story better. "Well, what idea did you get? I know you would've got one!"

"Oh, Mom." Her voice was apologetic. "It was silly, but all I could think of was to make baby blankets for babies in crisis."

I counteracted with instant approval. "That's a great idea!"

With a small laugh, she replied, "I didn't think so, because I already make fleece blankets for my family and friends, and they hardly seem like a big deal."

I sat down on the arm of the sofa in the lunchroom and leaned forward in all seriousness. "Well, what did you decide instead?"

"I couldn't think of anything else, so I eventually just wrote to make baby blankets for babies in crisis."

"Oh, good!" It seemed to me this was certainly the right decision.

She carried on explaining the process. "The next thing we had to do was put the card in the envelope provided, address it to ourselves and seal it. They'd mail them to us before next year's conference. It'll remind us of what we felt we were to do and hopefully have it done by then."

All the details of this challenge were impressive.

"The hardest part was that we were to go up to the front with our envelope and have a lady pray with us over our idea. I really didn't want to do that, but finally I convinced myself to get in line, anyway."

I was proud of Stephanie at that moment. It takes a lot of courage to be vulnerable with your idea, not knowing how someone else will view it.

"When it was my turn, I ended up in front of a lady named Brooke. I knew her sister Lisa, but I didn't know Brooke very well. She asked me what I had written. I told her it was a silly idea, nothing huge, but all I could think of was to make baby blankets for babies in crisis."

Feeling protective of her heart, I braced myself. "So, what was Brooke's reaction?"

"Mom, it was unbelievable!" Stephanie's voice rang with amazement. "She told me it was a great idea from her own personal experience."

I nodded my head, grinning. Not that she could see me, but my heart was grateful for the encouragement.

"I was so surprised to hear her say that." The relief and joy in Stephanie's voice was unmistakable. "Brooke reminded me that this past December she had preemie twins, a boy and a girl. She told me they had to stay in the hospital for nine weeks since they were so tiny and too premature to go home. She already had two small children at home and now added to her routine were constant trips back and forth to the hospital. It was a very stressful time for her and her family."

"I'm sure it was," I murmured sympathetically.

"Brooke said that volunteers at the hospital made knitted blankets for babies in the NICU. When she saw her little ones wrapped up in those blankets, she said they seemed to be swaddled in love. It encouraged her to know people cared about her babies. It was as if the blankets kept her babies safe and cared-for even when she wasn't with them."

I found it hard to get the words out past the lump in my throat, "Oh, Stephanie, that's amazing!! Brooke was the perfect person to connect with about your idea."

"Absolutely! She said other moms with babies in need will love my blankets! She prayed with me about it and now I have a plan." There was a sense of both peace and excitement in her voice, so I eagerly awaited the details.

"That's exciting! What's your plan?"

"I'm going to make ten baby blankets!"

Whoa, what a huge commitment.

Stephanie was still happily providing more details of her goal. "Five boy-themed blankets and five girl-themed ones. Even though I already have some fabric that might work, I'm going to look for the best material I can find. I'll make sure it's of high quality. I want to give those babies the best and softest blankets I can make!"

I knew Stephanie had an assortment of material at home, but to be so specific meant she had already thought this plan through.

As we said our goodbyes and I returned to my desk, I was simply in awe of how the conference challenge inspired Stephanie.

The next blanket-related phone call came three weeks later.

"Mom, I'm so excited 'cause they delivered some material today." Stephanie's excitement rang through loud and clear! "I ordered five unique patterns and colours in girly material. One side will be Minky and the other side flannel."

"What in the world is Minky?" I interrupted.

"Remember the Farmer's market we went to where I bought a blanket for Ava? I asked the vendor what type of fabric she had used, and she told me it was Minky material, so that's what I looked for online."

"So, Ava's giraffe-print and purple-coloured blanket is made of Minky material?"

"Yes. Minky is kind of expensive and difficult to find, but I kept checking the fabric stores as well and eventually found enough for the girl blankets. Even though it's pricey, to me that's all part of this challenge. I want this project to be significant in every way, including the cost to me."

"That fabric will make wonderful baby blankets. What kind of pattern will you follow?"

Stephanie laughed. "I found one on Pinterest."

"What in the world is Pinterest?" I was feeling quite out of touch with all this new jargon.

"It's a website. I hadn't heard of it until Kyle was telling us about all the decorating ideas he got for his wedding from Pinterest. I think it's hilarious that my own brother introduced me to it!"

She continued with a chuckle, "Anyway, it's amazing all the stuff you can learn on there. I found a tutorial for making baby blankets with a rolled hem. The fleece ones I usually make aren't overly fancy. This new way I've learned, though, will look so much nicer and more professional."

I had wondered about one other aspect of this project. "Stephanie, you said you wanted these blankets to go to babies in crisis. Do you have a place in mind to donate them?"

"Oh yeah! I should've told you I want them to go to the Pregnancy Care Centre since you and Dad are involved with the group, and I've been on their fund-raising walk-a-thons. I picture my blankets wrapped around babies whose teenage mothers decided to keep their babies, whose mothers were in crisis or simply needed extra support. Those are the babies I'm making these blankets for."

My daughter's compassionate heart blessed mine! "I'm proud of you, Stephanie. You're amazing!"

Since Stephanie had her own little girl, Ava, she made the girly blankets first. Then another excited phone call came, "Mom, you'll never believe what got delivered today."

"You're right. I've no idea!" I sat down at the kitchen table, preparing to be impressed.

"Do you remember the sewing labels I bought once that said, 'Made with love by Stephanie'?"

"Yes, I really liked the personalization."

"Well, I got special ones for these blankets. These labels are on silky smooth material, so they will be nice on baby skin."

"Hmmm, I'm fascinated. What's written on the label?"

"Well, there's no way I'd use a label with my name on it, so I looked online for a Bible verse with the words 'mercy and kindness' in it. I searched a lot of different translations before I found what I wanted."

This was intriguing to hear. "What verse did you find?"

"Let me read the label to you." With a bit of rustling of paper and plastic, Stephanie retrieved the labels.

> May the Lord bless and protect you and show you Mercy & Kindness.
> May he be good to you and give you peace. Numbers 6:24-26

"Stephanie," I choked out, "that's perfect for these blankets! I'm blown away!"

Stephanie finished the last of the boy blankets in spring of 2013. One more blanket-themed phone call came to me at work.

"Mom, would you be able to take me to the Pregnancy Care Centre tomorrow on your lunch break so that I can drop off these blankets?"

I felt honoured to be asked to join her on this delivery. "Yes! I'd be happy to!"

The next day, Stephanie met me at work with one more surprise. "Guess what was in the mail today?" Before I could respond, she blurted out, "My envelope from the conference!"

We both laughed at the timing of this reminder of her challenge. An entire year had already passed, and this was the last step in completing her pledge to God.

When we arrived at the centre, Stephanie reached into the backseat to get her promised blankets. As I took one pile of them, I couldn't help but stroke the soft Minky and colourful flannel. With great admiration I turned to her, "These are so wonderful, Stephanie."

"Thanks Mom. I wonder if Norah will be here today."

"If she is, that'd be great." Norah was the coordinator of the centre and a family friend.

We opened the front door and approached the reception desk.

"Hello. Is Norah here?"

"No, sorry, she's not in the office today. Can I help you?" The friendly staff member was unfamiliar to us.

Stephanie and I glanced at each other; disappointment reflected in our eyes. Stephanie stepped forward with her armload of blankets and held them out to the woman. I did the same.

"I came to drop these blankets off." She spoke hesitantly, with a slight crack in her voice. There was no mention of her making them, just the act of offering her gift of baby blankets as she had promised to God.

"That's great. Thank you very much." Donations of baby items were a regular occurrence at the centre. The woman took the blankets away to be absorbed into their inventory.

We felt deflated leaving the building. A void now existed at the finish of this challenge.

Stephanie voiced her feelings first. "I feel so weird, Mom. The blankets are gone, and I'll never know who will receive them. I know that's the whole point, but it feels so final and abrupt."

We walked side by side to the back parking lot. "It's a strange feeling, for sure." I agreed, trying to take the edge off our emotions. "Norah would've enjoyed the story behind the blankets' idea."

We stopped and turned towards each other. Our eyes widened as realization hit.

"Wait a minute," I burst out.

"Mom! The delivery went exactly as it was supposed to." Stephanie's words tumbled out at the same time.

With sudden clarity, I added, "You're right! Even though Norah wasn't the recipient of the blankets, it would've tarnished the whole concept of the challenge of doing something for others without recognition."

I reached over to give her a heartfelt hug. Stephanie looked at me, her eyes shimmering with tears and a determined resolve. "Yeah, but knowing ten babies will be swaddled in my blankets of mercy and kindness comforts me."

Blankets made because of a challenge accepted. Now, a mission accomplished.

A selfless act of love.

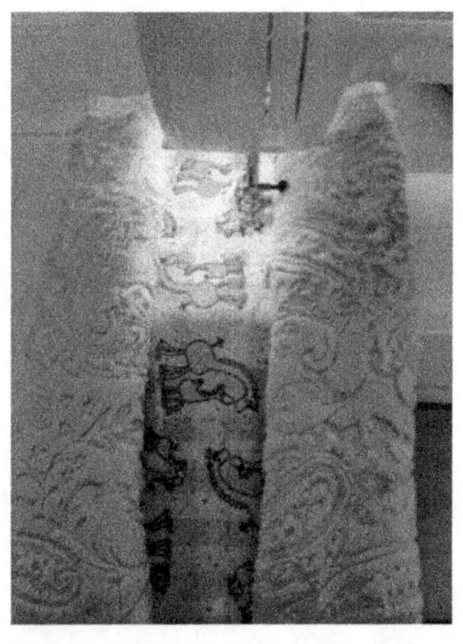

He is in Control

My youngest child, Ruth, announced she was taking a six-month Watoto Discipleship program in Kampala, Uganda. I was familiar with the Watoto Children's Choirs but knowing Ruth would go to a place we had no ties to was difficult to grasp. A million questions flooded my mind about feasibility, safety, health, and relationships. The description sounded good on paper, but my heart was concerned with the realities that she would face.

Ruth tackled the complicated application process and raised the money needed for an overseas program. Her determination helped her handle the culture shock, language barriers, and minority status when she arrived in Uganda. She was part of a houseful of other young women from around the world who were also in the program and served as a great support group.

During the discipleship program, Ruth fell in love with the land of red soil and its people. As her time there was coming to an end, a volunteer opportunity presented itself to help in one of the Watoto Children's Villages. This position would involve administrative duties, teaching, and visiting with house mothers. Ruth realized she wasn't ready to leave so she extended her stay another six months.

During this time, a traumatic ordeal tested her faith. Here is Ruth's account of the events, shared with her permission.

~~~~~~~~~~~~~~~~~~~~~~~

Thursday, October 23, 2014

I enthusiastically embarked on a shopping trip with my best friend Alice to downtown Kampala that morning. As a Lugandan-speaking Ugandan, Alice bartered a good deal for me, so I happily purchased pretty sandals and a new purse.

It was a lovely day however downtown Kampala was its usual mass chaos. Thousands of people flowed to and from shops, crammed into maze-like buildings and onto the sidewalks outside.
~~~~~~~~~~~~~~~~~~~~~~~

People flooded across the busy street for fresh food at the open market, dodging vehicles and bicycles coming from both directions. The babble of voices, shouts and whistles of vendors, horns beeping, and engines revving filled the air. A constant stream of people climbed aboard the matatus (public van taxis) and boda-bodas (motorcycle taxis).

Alice remained downtown to get her hair plaited, so I headed home through the maze of stores and out onto the street. Having lived in Kampala for ten months, it felt normal as I pushed my way through the crowds. Men tugged at my arms, and I pulled away, without so much as a glance in their direction. Other people shoved boxes of items for sale toward me and yelled "*Muzungu!*" (white person). Men uttered comments in Luganda, or English that I can't bring myself to repeat. Under a bright blue sky and brilliant sunshine, I trudged uphill on the heat-radiating sidewalk. I made it home with my new purchases, sweat running down my face. And yet, I smiled to myself. I had accomplished my morning mission and had the rest of the day to get ready to meet up with my friend Sam.

That evening, I felt wonderful wearing my new sandals and with my new purse hanging on my shoulder while Sam and I strolled through the mall. I glanced down at the ground and found a 20,000-shilling note (UGX) roughly worth $8 Canadian. This was great. The most I'd previously found was a 100-shilling coin (UGX) valued at 3 cents Canadian.

We ate out and went to the Teenage Mutant Ninja Turtles movie, then wandered over to Javas Coffee Shop for chai lattes and chocolate-fudge cake. Later, as we walked to the matatus to go to my home, I thought about how today was perfect and turned to Sam with a contented sigh. "This is our lucky day!" And well, it was.

It was 10:30 pm when we arrived at Watoto Church Central, the end of the local transit line, leaving us three more blocks to walk to my apartment. With no streetlights to illuminate the roads, we were thankful we knew our way. We laughed, talked, and enjoyed the last minutes of the evening, while making sure I wasn't late for my 11 o'clock curfew.

We passed by the dark and silent outdoor carwash on the corner and crossed the road to the next block. A walled compound bordered my left and Sam walked next to the paved road devoid of night traffic. We slowed down as I animatedly told Sam about how God brought me to a particular housemother's home in Bbira. As I turned to look at him my heart rose in my throat. A man appeared beside him. At first, I thought he must know Sam and jumped up to get his attention so we wouldn't pass by without greeting each other. I couldn't have been more wrong.

Silently and seemingly in one motion, this man leaped into the air, swung his leg up and around, and kicked Sam straight in the face with a powerful blow. Sam fell back, and I watched helplessly as his body starfished backwards, landing on the sidewalk with the assailant over top of him.

I tried to comprehend the scene in front of me as someone else from behind suddenly grabbed my new purse. I cried out as he swung around to my front and shoved me backwards, causing me to fall hard on the grassy area. Instinctively crossing my arms in an X, I refused to let him remove my purse from my left arm. He pulled back and forth on it five or six times until I heard a voice say, "Just let it go." I immediately realized that I was going to get hurt if I didn't let the purse go. I straightened my arms and let it slide off into the hands of the desperate Ugandan who then disappeared into the night.

From where I lay on the ground, I could see Sam a few feet away, his face covered in blood, but his assailant had also vanished. I struggled to my feet, calling out to him, "Sam, Sam! Are you okay?"

He sat up and rested his head on his knees as a security guard from the compound walked up to us, noting my tears and Sam's bloody face. The guard asked what was wrong, and I explained we had been robbed. He kept asking me where I had come from, and I kept stressing that the muggers ran down the street. He finally, slowly, moved in that direction.

Sam stared at me. "What did they take?"

When I mentioned my new purse, his next question was no surprise. "What was in it?"

I knew enough by now to limit what I carried in my purse, but it had held both my phones-an iPhone with my Canadian phone number and the Nokia flip-phone with my Ugandan number. Sam leapt to his feet and ran around the corner before I could say any more. Soon after, he stumbled and staggered back, unable to keep his balance. I encouraged him to sit down again while I tried to explain to another security guard from across the road that he should go after the muggers. The unarmed guard was not keen to pursue them.

Eventually, Sam and I stood up, holding on to each other to finish the walk to my apartment. We had to cross a large, unlit intersection just ahead of us. The dark frightened me more than ever and that intersection lurked with potential terror. We made it across the road without incident, but I was frantic to get help for Sam, who kept repeating, "I'm so sorry" as I literally dragged him along with me. Blood dripped from his swollen lip and nose. His confusion increased with every passing minute. He kept asking me what had happened. When we finally reached the grounds of my apartment, the guard didn't know me, and I had no way of proving that I lived in this building. Finally, after pleading and crying, the guard opened the compound gate and let us in. I had to ring the doorbell for my roommates, as my house key was in my stolen purse. When the door opened, I promptly burst into tears again.

We took Sam to a doctor who simply treated his cuts. I asked the doctor if he thought Sam had a concussion. He concluded there was no concussion since he hadn't vomited. He sent us home without providing painkillers. Upon arriving back at my apartment, Sam threw up. We realized we couldn't let him sleep, so all night we kept waking him to check on him. Sam's confusion and memory loss increased over the next day, even after we got him back to his home. He knew my name but did not know how we knew each other.

Our friends and his family, who rallied around us, blessed us. They helped with transportation, meals, and encouragement over the following days.

On Sunday, Richard, one of my former leaders from my 360 Discipleship Program, came to check on us. He had everyone in the room hold hands, forming a circle around Sam who lay on his couch, and we prayed.

Richard also prayed for the two men who attacked us. I remember opening my eyes, staring at him, thinking, "What?!" Not that I was upset he was praying for them, but I hadn't thought twice about them. I couldn't picture their faces or what they were wearing. In my memory they were simply two moving, violent, frantic beings.

I heard many more stories of muggings while I was in Uganda, most of which were far more violent and tragic than ours. I don't know why these things happen, but when people are desperate, they do desperate things. As I pondered this, my heart broke for this country, and for these two men. What must their life be like that made them live in the shadows and prey on people who pass by? May God have mercy on them.

Later that week, I woke up with an urgency to read a specific part of my Bible. I turned to Psalm 139 which reassures us God is always with us, no matter where we are. Verses 11 and 12 spoke to my fear of the dark after being mugged:

If I say, "Surely the darkness will hide me, and the light become night around me, even the darkness will not be dark to you; the night will shine like the day, for darkness is as light to you."

The darkness was as day to God. He was there with us. His angels were there, too. God was in control.

The next chapter I read was about David hiding from his enemies and crying out to God for justice and mercy. Psalm 140:1-8 resonated with me as never before:

Rescue me, Lord, from evildoers;
protect me from the violent,
who devise evil plans in their hearts
and stir up war every day.
They make their tongues as sharp as a serpent's;
the poison of vipers is on their lips.

Keep me safe, Lord, from the hands of the wicked;
protect me from the violent,
who devise ways to trip my feet.
The arrogant have hidden a snare for me;
they have spread out the cords of their net
and have set traps for me along my path.

I say to the Lord, you are my God.
Hear Lord, my cry for mercy.
Sovereign Lord, my strong deliverer,
you shield my head in the day of battle.

> Do not grant the wicked their desires, Lord;
> do not let their plans succeed.

These words amazed me. I could now relate personally to them.

> Protect me from the violent who devise ways
> to trip my feet.

That man literally tripped my feet.

> They have set traps for me along my path.

They did that too!

> I say to the Lord, you are my God. Hear Lord,
> my cry for mercy. Sovereign Lord, my strong
> deliverer, you shield my head in the day of
> battle.

I repeated my story many times throughout that week and each time I talked about the voice I heard, it was clear it couldn't have been the assailant as I'd initially thought. While in the chaos of that mugging, it was as if I was momentarily in the eye of the storm. I heard a calm, kind, and steady voice say, "Just let it go." I knew I simply had to obey.

Suddenly, it clicked. It wasn't the mugger who said anything. It was God speaking to me. The Lord had heard my cry! God spoke to me in that moment of confusion, terror, and shock. He spoke, and I listened.

It was a lucky day, a blessed day. The outcome could have been so much worse. What happened was not okay. But we would be okay. Sam's memory gradually returned. His facial cuts healed. The bruises on my arm reminded me of what I had been through, but as those bruises faded, so did the shock and trauma.

My God is in control, and I will continue to hold on to that with all my might.

Uganda is not an evil place. It's not filled with evil people. However, Uganda, like every other nation in the world, has its share of hurting and lost people. It's also filled with caring, compassionate, loving people, such as the ones who supported Sam and I through this ordeal.

Every day became a little better, a little brighter, a little easier. For that, I'm grateful, so very grateful. My God loves me and cares for me. He watches over me.

~~~~~~~~~~~~~~~~~~~~~~

Hearing from Ruth about the mugging, I was very thankful she had not been more seriously hurt or killed. When life happens beyond our control or reach, knowing God was as close to
~~~~~~~~~~~~~~~~~~~~~~

Ruth in Uganda as here in Canada comforted my heart.

Ruth's second trip to Uganda was eight years later, for her second wedding anniversary with her husband, Simon. They met in Edmonton, where they discovered they had Uganda in common, as Simon was born there. This trip was to meet the rest of Simon's family and see where he grew up.

Before flying back home to Edmonton, Ruth briefly saw the places where she lived, was mugged, and had grown in her faith. The flood of memories served as a reminder that God has always been in control.

Previous hurt and fear were replaced by the warmth and welcome of a kind and loving family. A family who helped raise Simon to become the gentle and devoted husband he is to our Ruth.

Thank you, God, for your love and faithful care in all of life's circumstances.

First time in Uganda

Second time in Uganda, with Simon

Honey's Bears

Each step felt heavier than the last as I climbed the steep outdoor staircase to Mum Stewart's former apartment. It was May 2008 when my daughters, Heather, Ruth, and Stephanie along with Stephanie's new hubby Adam, joined me in Brantford, Ontario, for Mum Stewart's funeral. Peter arrived earlier in the week and had the privilege of being with his Mum as she drew her last breath and slipped quietly away to heaven.

As I opened the door to her little second-floor apartment tucked up under the roof, I took a deep breath, bracing myself for the emptiness. Although Mum had lived in a senior's residence for the past year, I had never seen her there. I could only picture Mum in this lovely little home above her son Doug and his wife Karen's place, where she lived for almost ten years. Most of Mum's personal belongings were gone, but some basic furniture remained in the apartment. I went through the four rooms *seeing* Mum in every one of them. My heart ached with sorrow and the love I always had for my dear Mum-in-law.

Peter and I would stay in her bedroom this time, which only emphasized her absence. I went to the back of her room to hang clothes from my suitcase. The handle clicked, and the door swung open. To my amazement, a short fur coat hung in an otherwise empty closet. Mum's husband, Victor, who passed away before I became his daughter-in-law, had given her this jacket many, many years before.

I immediately knew I wanted to have this jacket, and I knew what I wanted to do with it.

During our time in Ontario, we shared priceless family time together, celebrating this wonderful Mum of ours. With fresh memories tucked in our hearts, it was time to go our separate ways. The family easily agreed to the coat coming home with me as we headed back to Edmonton, Alberta.

The fur jacket hung in my closet until February the next year, when John Godfrey, a friend from northern BC, arrived in town. His visit prompted me to act on my idea for the jacket. I phoned

Lynnette Gullackson, a dear friend in Fort Nelson, the place where we lived fifteen years earlier.

Hearing Lynnette's voice again was as delightful as flowers blooming in spring. We spent some time updating each other on our lives before I broached the reason for my call.

"When Peter and I stayed at Mum Stewart's old apartment for the funeral, I came across her fur jacket. It instantly reminded me of when your mother died shortly after we had moved to Fort Nelson."

There was a brief pause before Lynnette warmly responded. "You mean when I made teddy bears out of my mom's long fur coat?"

"Yes! You told me your maiden-name was Brown, and you made seven 'Little Brown Bears' for you and your siblings. I was amazed at your creativity that turned something no longer practical into something to treasure." Taking a deep breath, I added. "I'm wondering if you would consider making three little bears out of Mum Stewart's jacket for me. They wouldn't need to be ready until Christmas time."

I held my breath as I waited for Lynnette's reply.

"Real fur is tricky to work with."

I braced myself for her gentle refusal.

"But I'll consider it because we knew your Mum when she visited while you were in Fort Nelson with us."

I exhaled loudly even as happiness washed over me. "Lynnette, I'm so grateful that you'd even consider it."

I breathed a sigh of relief and a prayer of thanks to God for Lynnette's willingness. "I have the perfect way to get the coat to you since John Godfrey is in the city on business. He'll be at our church tomorrow so I'm sure he'll take the coat back with him."

"That sounds like a great plan. Send it along and I'll look at the jacket to determine if the fur is in good enough condition to work with. I'll get back to you after I've checked it out."

As I hung up the phone, I could hardly contain my excitement. My idea seemed a hopeful possibility!

Upon receiving the jacket, Lynnette let me know after her examination that the fur was in decent condition. She felt certain she could make three small bears with the amount of fur she had to work with.

It wasn't until early September when I received a teddy-bear-related phone call.

"Hello Melody. I finished the three bears this week, but I have a question for you. Do you want to name them yourself, or would you like me to do that?"

I laughed, "Lynnette, I never even thought about names. Please do that for me as you have such wonderful creativity in naming all the bears you made over the years!"

"Okay, I'll do that and ship the bears to your place tomorrow."

When at long last the three bears arrived at my home, I was as excited as a kid at Christmas. I held my breath as I opened the flaps of the box. There they were. Three beautiful reddish-brown fur bears that had once been a jacket handled and worn by Mum Stewart.

After examining each bear and adjusting their moveable arms, legs, and heads just so, I set them on my table to look closely at their name tags. Each of the bears wore a sage green bow around its neck made from the coat's lining. Attached to the bow was a little handmade card, giving me the details of the bears.

The gold embossed bear on the front of the card had "Teddy Treasures by Lynnette" written next to it.

Inside each card was the following hand-written information:

Made of Vintage Mink
Hand-blown German glass eyes
Filled with polyfill & plastic pellets
Leather nose
Made by
Lynnette Gullackson
Not suitable for small children

The back of each card revealed their names - Faith, Hope and Charity. How perfect!

Unknown to them, my two sisters-in-law would each be the recipients of a bear, and one was for me.

"Faith Bear" was perfect for Sharon, as her faith in God has always been paramount throughout her life.

"Hope Bear" became mine as a reminder that my God of hope is always with me.

"Charity Bear" simply had to go to Karen, as Mum Stewart had lived with them for so many years. Karen's love for Mum was evident in her care for her until the end of her days. Charity came with a little extra piece of memorabilia. Lynnette had made a drawstring pouch from a pocket in the lining, which had Mum Stewart's initials embroidered on it.

MWS-Muriel Winifred Stewart.

Three daughters-in-law who loved their "Mum" would now have a unique reminder of that bond. I know that Mum Stewart would have heartily approved of her jacket becoming three adorable little bears! Such a wonderful treasure was hanging in that closet, just waiting to be found.

~~~~~~~~~~~~~~~~~~~~~~~

My middle daughter, Heather, had a special bond with her Grandma Stewart. When Heather was learning to talk, Grandma called her "Honey" and so that's what Heather called her back. It was extremely cute to hear Heather call out "Hi Honey" to Mum when we visited.

Heather's love for her grandma was so strong that she chose Mum Stewart's birthday for Daniel and her to be married on, five years after Mum passed away.

Their firstborn was a son, named Roman. A couple of years later, Heather gave birth to a little girl whom she wanted to name after her beloved Grandma. The problem was that grandma's names didn't really suit until Heather
~~~~~~~~~~~~~~~~~~~~~~~

thought about her "pet name" Honey. Simply perfect!

They named their daughter Lillian Honey Quebec after "Honey" Muriel Winifred Stewart.

When we were planning Lillian's baby shower, it was easy to decide on the theme of honey and bees for decorations. Nestled amid jars of honey, sat a beautiful little bear called Hope.

Someday, when our Lillian Honey is grown up, she will learn the story of how her namesake, Great-Grandma Honey's fur coat turned into three little bears.

Muriel Stewart in her fur coat.

Faith, Hope and Charity Bears.

Invisible Threads

The ringing of the house phone startled me. I'd been lost in thought gazing out into the backyard as I dried dishes. Kyle's name appeared on the call display, and I wiped my hands on the tea towel draped over my shoulder, smiling as I lifted the receiver to my ear.

"Hi Mom. Sorry I didn't call you on your birthday."

"That's okay, Kyle. It was a busy evening with your sisters and Adam here for dinner. Tonight's a better time to talk."

Kyle had a smile and a hint of mystery in his voice. "I have a good excuse. I was on a date. Kind of."

I was suddenly and intensely all ears. Kyle seemed willing to talk about his kind-of date. *Don't overreact. Keep your cool.*

Hoping my voice sounded nonchalant even with my curiosity on high alert, I replied, "Oooooh, that's interesting."

With a laugh, Kyle continued. "My friends Geoff and Naomi were going to a youth group girl's birthday party. I wasn't officially invited but Geoff said I had to go with them to her house."

I was sitting on the edge of my chair, leaning into the phone, ensuring I'd not miss a single word he seemed willing to share. "And?"

"Well, they convinced me. After being there for a while, I went to the kitchen for a drink and recognized a girl from church. We'd only said hi before, but this time, we started talking. She didn't plan to stay long since she was working on her master's degree in audiology and had to study, but she wanted to show up for her friend."

"Wow, that's cool! Then what happened?"

"Nothing much because she left soon after that, but when I got home, I emailed her some information that we'd talked about. She answered, so I emailed back and asked to meet for coffee."

I exhaled the breath I didn't realize I was holding. "How did that go?"

"We met up at a coffee shop and picked up where we left off. Besides the hour and a half there, we kept talking longer in the parking lot. We have so much in common, it's almost scary," he acknowledged. "Her family has three girls and one boy like our family. She's moved around a lot, so she doesn't like it either when people ask her where she's from."

I smiled. This was something Kyle disliked about his life. He usually avoided the answer, as it was too complicated.

"Her dad's a pastor, like Dad, but right now, her parents are missionaries somewhere."

I sat up straight in the chair in surprise. My mind reeled with questions. "What country are her parents' missionaries in?"

"I don't remember. It might be Thailand, but I'm not sure."

I couldn't think of any missionaries I knew in Thailand, but Kyle continued. "Her name is Danielle, but her family calls her Danni with two 'ns'."

An interesting abbreviation. "What's her last name?"

"Winsor." He emphasized that Winsor didn't have a "d."

"Danielle grew up in Newfoundland." We also had family connections with that province.

"Oh yeah, one more thing. She was born in Taiwan."

"*Taiwan*!!" burst out of me before I could stop it. My heart pounded. "When your dad was in Taiwan, he stayed with a family named Winsor part of the time. I wonder if it was them?"

I covered the mouthpiece of the telephone handset and yelled down the hall to Peter in his office, "*Peter!* Those missionaries in Taiwan, the Winsors, what's their first names?"

His response wasn't immediate as he processed what I was asking. "Gary and Eva. Why?"

"I'm talking to Kyle, and he met a girl who might be related." I explained as I uncovered the mouthpiece and asked, "Are Danielle's parents' names Gary and Eva?"

The question caught Kyle off guard. "I've no idea. We just had one date!"

I chuckled, as if it was no big deal. "Well, make sure you ask her next time you talk. Wouldn't that be something?!"

"I'll try to remember. That would be even weirder if it's them."

Our conversation wound down, but the excitement in my mind grew. My heart raced with the possibility that this was not an accidental connection!

I hung up the phone and hurried down the hall to Peter's office to convey all the details of this fascinating conversation. While I talked, I scanned the books on his bookshelf to find his journal from Taiwan. There it was with a grey striped cover and black spine.

Peter escaped the office and my boisterous enthusiasm as I sat down at the desk and skimmed through the journal. I scanned for any mention of the name Winsor or Danni. Peter's first mention of meeting Gary Winsor was four days after arriving in Taiwan in late October 1990. He had stayed with Gary and Eva for a week in November.

One day at the English class Eva led, Peter let it slip that it was his thirty-sixth birthday, so the ladies rushed out and bought a cake. That evening before the prayer meeting our kids and I phoned him from Canada to wish him a happy birthday. After service, the Winsors and their neighbours also had cake to celebrate his day. A very notable birthday for him.

During his time at their apartment, Peter fixed three doors, so they'd close properly. He also played racquetball twice with Gary and Eva. During one of those game times, their daughters, Lynette, and Danni, accompanied them.

The Winsors drove Peter to the airport to fly home to Canada. The clincher came in the last entry of the journal written in Taipei, Taiwan, December 16, 1990; twenty years earlier:

> I had the suitcase all packed - with the help of Danni (age 4 1/2).

It was hard to grasp all the connections scrawled across the pages of this journal. It seemed a certainty the Winsors would remember Peter's visit even now. I closed the book, already knowing in my heart these circumstances had all the earmarks of being a God-thing. Perhaps this could become a "happily-ever-after" kind of story. Confirmation of the connection was all I needed to know.

I sat in the office, smiling to myself, savouring all the information Kyle had shared. It was in that moment God reminded me of a sulky one-sided conversation I'd had with Him earlier.

I missed Kyle, who had been living away from home the previous few years. He had taken college courses in British Columbia and Ontario and now lived in British Columbia working on a degree. He was part of a youth group at the Ladner Pentecostal church and had made friends, but my thoughts spiraled into a pity party of my own making. I was sure he would fall in love with a young lady from BC. They'd get married, and he'd become absorbed into her family over there and I'd rarely ever see him. I missed him here in our world in Edmonton, Alberta. I was feeling sorry for myself and thought God should hear about it.

I closed my eyes and bowed my head. "God, I'm sorry. I should know better than to expect the worst-case scenario. I should trust you more. You've always proven how much you care. You have amazing ways of working things out. Thank you for the hope this phone call has given me. No matter the outcome."

Kyle called back on the weekend. "Well Mom, you'll be interested to know Danielle and I went on an official date this week."

I fist-pumped the air at this good news!

"I even remembered to ask her parent's names and yes, they're Gary and Eva Winsor. Danielle doesn't remember dad. She was too young when he was there."

My heart and feet did a happy dance as tears of amazement stung my eyes.

~~~~~~~~~~~~~~~~~~~~~~~

Six weeks after that phone call, Peter and I drove to the lower mainland to help Kyle move to a different apartment and to meet this young lady. As Peter moved the car closer to Kyle's entrance, another car pulled in, facing him. A young woman exited the vehicle.

Peter recognized her instantly. He quickly got out of the car and walking toward her stated matter-of-factly, "Hello. You must be Danielle. You look just like your mother did when I stayed at your place in Taiwan."

"I get that a lot," Danielle laughed. "You must be Peter. It's nice to meet you. Again."

~~~~~~~~~~~~~~~~~~~~~~~

Kyle and Danielle did indeed tie the matrimonial knot in January 2012. Now with a family of three boys, Ira, Francis, and Elliot, they live in Alberta, a mere 5-hour drive from our home. Instead of "losing" my son, I gained a wonderful daughter-in-law whose first connection to our family happened long before I ever met her.

Epilogue:

Two years after Kyle and Danielle were married, her parents came to visit them and us in Alberta. The Winsors were now missionaries in Hong Kong, returning to Ontario for vacation time. Before they arrived at our home, I found a small journal of my mother's. One section with a tab marked "Pray" caught my attention. This is one of her entries I showed the Winsors:

> February 28, 1988
> Pray for Gary Winsor in Taiwan. He has a good way of leading those people to the Lord.

My mother wrote this when Kyle was almost five and Danielle was two.

How amazed she would be to know her very own grandson married that missionary's daughter twenty-four years later.

Feb 28/85 - Gary Winsor in Taiwan -

Mom's prayer focus – 1988

Danielle and Kyle January 2012

The In-Laws
Gary & Eva Winsor – Melody & Peter Stewart

Weaving in the Ends

It's easy to dismiss the little moments in life as not important but, when the "warp and weave yarns" connect and the big picture appears, there is no mistaking that God cares about the tiniest details of our lives.

For many months I searched various online sites for a suitable weaving picture for my book cover. None came close to what I wanted, even with the publishing deadline weighing down on me.

My summer break destination was to my sister Sandra's home a thousand kilometers away. On our last evening together, while tying up loose ends of multiple conversations, Sandra casually brought out a length of material to show me. She planned to use it to recover an antique rocking chair.

I jumped up to examine it. "That's it! The perfect example of weaving I want for the cover of my book!"

Up close, the weaving lines are clearly visible.
From a distance, the pattern and colours
create a beautiful design.
The dark strands are vital in making the bright colours stand out.
Another example of God in the details.

The fabric of our faith is woven over time. It is spun through exciting, wonderful times, deep-sorrowing times, and just ordinary everyday times. Seeing the hand of God in all the details of these stories, strengthens my faith and keeps me moving forward.

My heart's desire is that my children, their children, and future generations will walk in similar footsteps of faith. When they look at the imprints they've left behind, may their life stories record the goodness of God woven in the details of their lives.

May God bless each of you on your own journey.

Melody

ABOUT THE AUTHOR

Melody is a debut author with an innate ability to recognize connections God creates in our world. What most people see as a coincidence, Melody sees as a God thing.

Born in Ontario, Canada, Melody grew up in a strong Christian family. From an early age she experienced and noticed God's personal involvement in people's lives. Her desire to share these connections has grown with the passing years.

As a pastor's wife, she lived in several locations with her husband Peter and four children. Her family has now expanded to include spouses and precious grandchildren.

Melody continues to watch God weave the threads used to connect us all in his beautiful tapestry.